Crochet
GIFTS

pil

Publications International, Ltd.

Consulting by Heidi Beazley

Written by Beth Taylor

Photo styling by Jessi Ledonne and Amy Stark

Photography by Christopher Hiltz, except pages 4, 6, 10 from Shutterstock.com

Crochet symbols and abbreviations from Craft Yarn Council's www.YarnStandards.com

Louis Weber, CEO
Publications International, Ltd.
8140 Lehigh Avenue
Morton Grove, IL 60053

ISBN: 978-1-68022-490-0

Manufactured in China.

8 7 6 5 4 3 2 1

Table of Contents

What You'll Need

Crochet Hooks

Crochet hooks can be made from aluminum, plastic, wood, or bamboo. They are available in a wide range of sizes and are used with an assortment of yarns. Steel hooks are the smallest and are often used with fine thread in delicate crochet work, such as lace and doilies. Most patterns and yarn labels recommend a hook size. Select a crochet hook that feels comfortable to you and works well with your project and yarn.

Common Hook Sizes

U.S.	B-1	C-2	D-3	E-4	F-5	G-6	7	H-8	I-9	J-10	K-10.5	L-11	M-13	N-15	P	Q	S
mm	2.25	2.75	3.25	3.5	3.75	4	4.5	5	5.5	6	6.5	8	9	10	15	16	19

Needles

Tapestry or yarn needles have a blunt tip and an eye large enough to accommodate thick yarns. These special needles can be used to weave in yarn ends or sew crocheted pieces together.

Stitch Markers

As their name suggests, stitch markers are designed to mark your stitches. They can be used to mark a certain number of stitches, the beginning of a round, or where to make a particular stitch. Stitch markers must have openings so that they can be easily removed. You can purchase stitch markers, or improvise with pins, earrings, or safety pins.

Pins

Use long, rustproof pins for blocking and pinning seams together. Pins can also serve as stitch markers. Opt for pins with large, colorful heads that won't get lost in your crochet work.

Measurement Tools

Measuring tape is a must-have tool when taking body measurements before making garments. Measuring tape and rulers can be used to measure gauge.

All About Yarn

Yarn for Beginners

Before starting any new crochet project, you must select your yarn. For beginners learning the basic stitches, select a simple cotton yarn that is light colored, smooth, and sturdy. It's harder to see your stitches with dark colored yarn. Avoid fuzzy and loosely woven yarns that fray easily.

Yarn Fibers

Natural fibers

Cotton, linen, and hemp yarns are made from plant fibers. They are lightweight, breathable, and machine washable. Mercerized cotton has undergone a chemical process that results in stronger, shinier yarn.

Yarns made from animal fibers include wool, silk, cashmere, mohair, alpaca, and angora. These animal fibers are much warmer than plant fibers. Both natural fibers offer a bit of stretch.

Synthetic fibers

Yarns made from synthetic fibers include nylon, rayon, acrylic, and polyester. Synthetic yarns are usually less expensive than natural fibers, but are less breathable and pill more easily.

Novelty and specialty yarns

Novelty and specialty yarns can be tricky to work with, but create a distinctive look. They include bouclé, ladder, eyelash, and chenille. While great for trims and accessories, novelty yarn is not best for beginners.

Selecting Your Yarn

Each package of store-bought yarn has a label listing the yarn's length, fiber content, and weight. Yarn weight refers to the thickness of a yarn. It ranges from the thinnest embroidery thread to the bulkiest yarn. Yarn labels also recommend hook size—just look for the crochet hook symbol to find the U.S. and metric hook size.

Yarn Weight Guidelines

LACE 0

Yarn types: Fingering, lace, and 10-count crochet thread
Recommended hook sizes (metric): 1.5–2.25 mm
Recommended hook sizes (U.S.): Steel 6 to B–1
Crochet gauge range: 32–42 double crochet stitches to 4 in.

SUPER FINE 1

Yarn types: Sock, fingering, and baby
Recommended hook sizes (metric): 2.25–3.5 mm
Recommended hook sizes (U.S.): B–1 to E–4
Crochet gauge range: 21–32 single crochet stitches to 4 in.

FINE 2

Yarn types: Sport and baby
Recommended hook sizes (metric): 3.5–4.5 mm
Recommended hook sizes (U.S.): E–4 to 7
Crochet gauge range: 16–20 single crochet stitches to 4 in.

LIGHT 3

Yarn types: Double knitting and light worsted
Recommended hook sizes (metric): 4.5–5.5 mm
Recommended hook sizes (U.S.): 7 to I–9
Crochet gauge range: 12–17 single crochet stitches to 4 in.

MEDIUM 4

Yarn types: Afghan, aran, and worsted
Recommended hook sizes (metric): 5.5–6.5 mm
Recommended hook sizes (U.S.): I–9 to K–10.5
Crochet gauge range: 11–14 single crochet stitches to 4 in.

BULKY 5

Yarn types: Chunky, craft, and rug
Recommended hook sizes (metric): 6.5–9 mm
Recommended hook sizes (U.S.): K–10.5 to M–13
Crochet gauge range: 8–11 single crochet stitches to 4 in.

SUPER BULKY 6

Yarn types: Bulky and roving
Recommended hook sizes (metric): 9–15 mm
Recommended hook sizes (U.S.): M–13 to Q
Crochet gauge range: 7–9 single crochet stitches to 4 in.

JUMBO 7

Yarn types: Jumbo and roving
Recommended hook sizes (metric): 15 mm and larger
Recommended hook sizes (U.S.): Q and larger
Crochet gauge range: 6 single crochet stitches and fewer to 4 in.

Source: Craft Yarn Council's www.YarnStandards.com

Choosing Yarn Colors

When selecting yarn for a crochet project, it's helpful to know a few basics about the color wheel and some harmonizing color schemes.

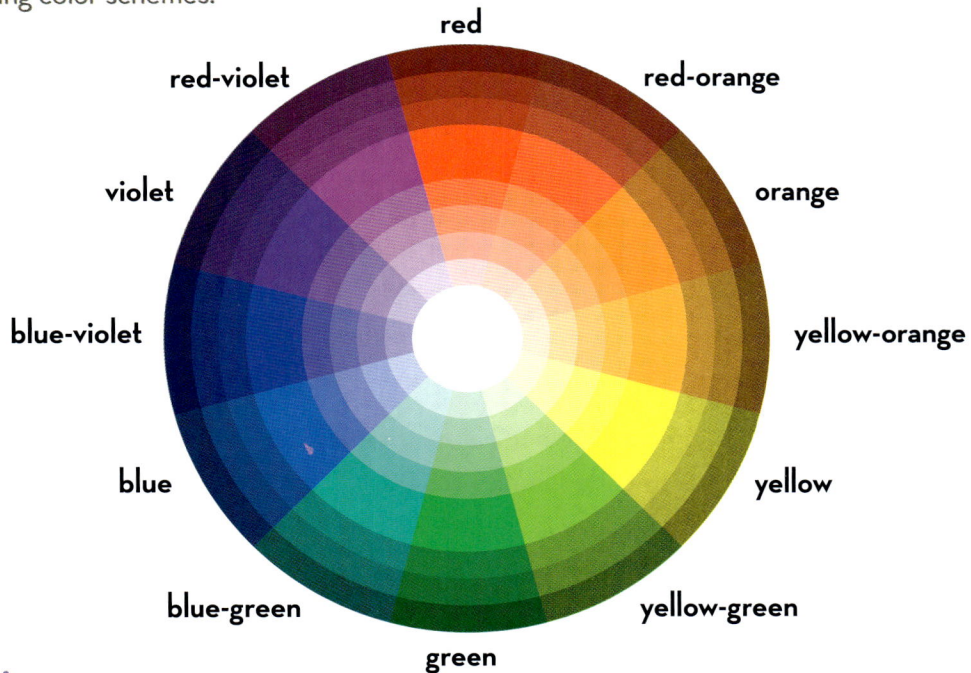

Color Schemes

Monochromatic

Monochromatic color schemes are based on one color. They use variations in value (lightness or darkness) and intensity (brightness or dullness) of a single color.

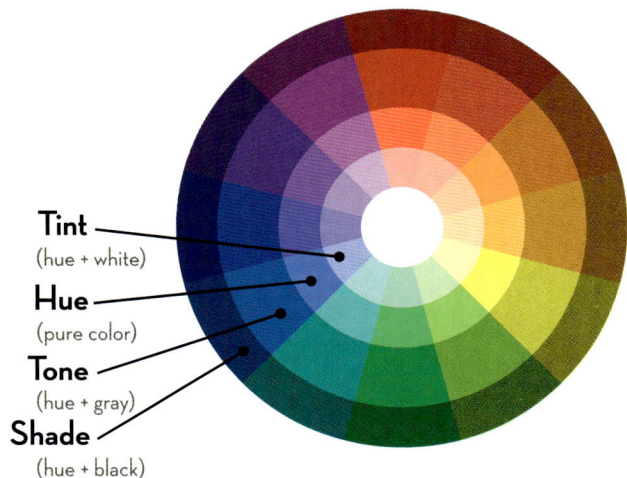

Tint
(hue + white)

Hue
(pure color)

Tone
(hue + gray)

Shade
(hue + black)

Analogous

Analogous color schemes use colors that are adjacent to each other on the color wheel (e.g., blue-violet, blue, blue-green). While similar to monochromatic schemes, analogous schemes offer more nuances. Typically one color is chosen as a dominant color and the others are used as accent colors.

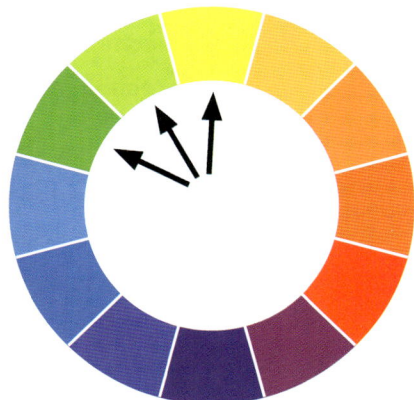

Complementary

Complementary color schemes use two colors that are directly opposite of each other on the color wheel (e.g., orange and blue; red and green). This scheme contrasts a warm color (yellow, yellow-orange, orange, red-orange, red, or red-violet) with a cool color (violet, blue-violet, blue, blue-green, green, or yellow-green).

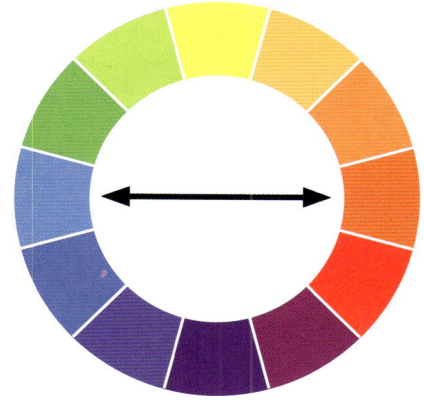

Split Complementary

Split complementary schemes use a color and the two colors adjacent to its complement (e.g., yellow, red-violet, blue-violet; red-violet, green, yellow). Try using a single warm color against a range of cool colors. This puts the emphasis on the warm color.

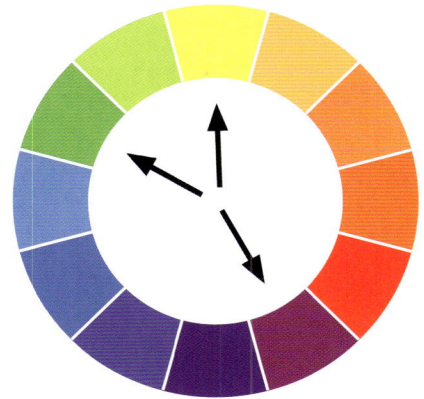

Triadic

Triadic color schemes use three colors equally spaced around the color wheel (e.g., orange, green, and violet; red-orange, blue-violet, and yellow-green). On a twelve-color wheel, selecting every fourth color on the wheel would make a triadic scheme.

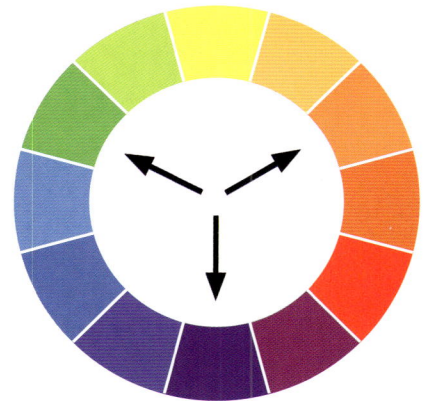

Tetradic (Double Complementary)

Tetradic, or double complementary, schemes use four colors. Two complementary color pairs make up the four colors (e.g., yellow, violet, blue, orange). Avoid using pure colors in equal amounts. This scheme looks best when one color is dominant and the others are more muted.

The Basics

Holding the Hook

Pencil Hold

Knife Hold

or

Tip: The instructions and photographs in this book are intended for right-handed crocheters. If you are a lefty, try holding up a mirror to the edge of a photograph to see the left-handed version.

Holding the Yarn

1

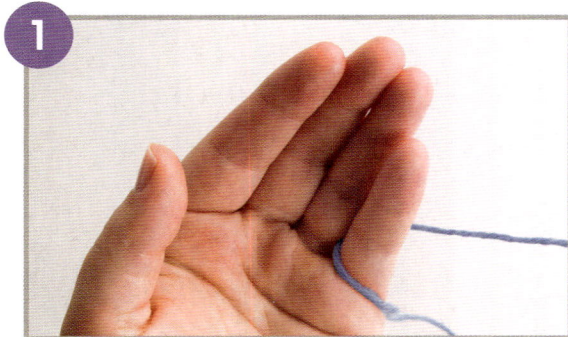

With your palm facing up, weave the working yarn (the yarn coming from the ball) between your pinky and ring fingers. Wrap the yarn clockwise around your pinky.

2

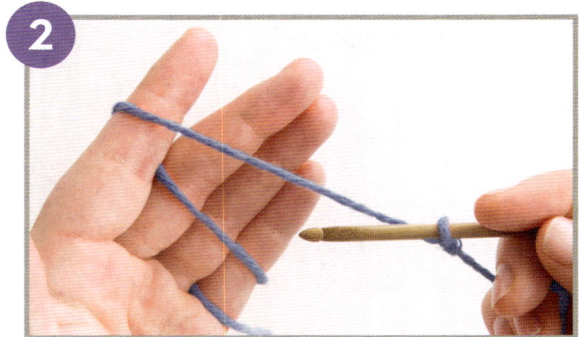

Take the yarn across your ring and middle fingers. Then wrap the yarn under and around your index finger.

3

Hold the yarn under the slip knot with your left thumb and middle finger.

Tip: There are many ways to hold your yarn. Experiment with different methods until you find what is most comfortable for you.

Making a Slip Knot

The first step in any crochet project is a slip knot.
The slip knot is what attaches the yarn to your hook.

1

Wrap the yarn around your index and middle fingers on your yarn hand to create an X.

2

From the top, insert your hook under the first loop to grab the second loop.

3

Draw the second loop you just grabbed under and up through the first loop.

4

Slide your fingers out. Pull your hook up while gently pulling both ends of the yarn down.

5

Pull the ends of the yarn to tighten the slip knot close to your hook.

6

With a finished slip knot around your hook, you are ready to start crocheting.

Chain Stitch (ch)

Crochet often begins with a series of chain stitches used to make up the first row. This is called the foundation chain and is the basic start to most crochet projects.

1

Start with a slip knot on your hook. Hold the yarn tail for tension.

2

yarn over

slip knot

Bring the working yarn (the yarn coming from the ball) over your hook from back to front. This is called yarn over (yo).

3

Draw this section of yarn back through the slip knot. You will have 1 new loop on your hook when your first chain stitch is complete.

4

Yarn over again.

5

Draw this section of yarn through the loop on your hook. You will have 1 new loop on your hook each time you complete a chain stitch.

6

Repeat steps 2–3 until your foundation chain has the required number of chain stitches.

Tension

Tension keeps your stitches neat and consistent. Make sure the chains in your foundation chain are even and loose enough to allow your hook back into those chains for the next row.

Too loose

Too tight

Just right

Slip Stitch (sl st)

The slip stitch is one of the most basic crochet stitches and is often used for joining.

Start with a foundation chain on your hook. Insert your hook from front to back into the second chain from your hook. There are 2 loops on your hook.

Yarn over, bringing the working yarn over your hook from back to front.

Draw the yarn through both loops on your hook. You will have 1 new loop on your hook when your first slip stitch is complete.

Counting Chains

Crochet patterns usually begin by telling you the number of chains needed for the foundation chain.

Identifying the Front and Back

The front of the foundation chain looks like a braid with a series of Vs. The back side of the foundation chain has a vertical ridge of bumps running down the middle from your hook to the end of the chain. Count chains from the front side.

Front

Back

Counting

Begin counting from the top of the foundation chain. (You can also count from the bottom up.) Do not count the loop on your hook or the slip knot on the bottom. Count only completed, V-shaped chain stitches. This example has 13 completed chain stitches.

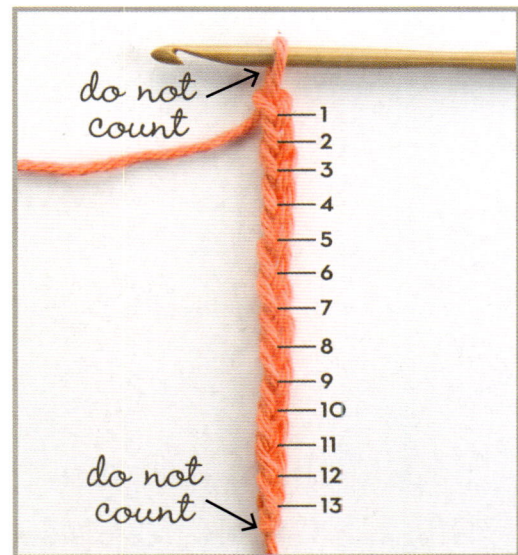

do not count

1
2
3
4
5
6
7
8
9
10
11
12
13

do not count

Tip: When creating a long foundation chain, it is helpful to use stitch markers every 10 or 20 stitches to make counting easier.

Turning Chains (tch)

Stitch	Number of Turning Chains
Single crochet	1
Half double crochet	2
Double crochet	3
Treble crochet	4

Each of the 4 basic crochet stitches requires a specific number of turning chains at the beginning or end of a row. The number of extra stitches neeed for the turning chain is added to the number needed for the foundation chain.

Single Crochet (sc)

How to single crochet:

To begin a row of single crochet, first stitch a foundation chain to the desired length. Add 1 extra chain stitch for the turning chain.

1

insert your hook into this stitch

Insert your hook from front to back into the second chain stitch from your hook. There will now be 2 loops on your hook.

2

Yarn over. Draw this yarn through the first loop on your hook. There will be 2 loops on your hook.

3

Yarn over again and draw this yarn through both loops on your hook. You will have 1 loop remaining on your hook when your first single crochet is complete.

4

insert your hook into this stitch

Insert your hook into the next chain stitch. Repeat steps 2–3 to complete another single crochet stitch.

5

Repeat step 4, working a single crochet stitch into each chain. At the end of the row, make 1 chain stitch for the turning chain.

6

insert your hook into this stitch

Turn your work so that the opposite side faces you. Insert your hook into the first single crochet stitch of the previous row and repeat steps 2–3. (Skip the turning chain.)

7

Insert your hook into the next stitch and repeat steps 2–3, working a single crochet stitch into each single crochet of the previous row.

8

Repeat step 7 to continue the pattern. At the end of all rows, chain 1 for the turning chain, turn, and insert your hook into the next stitch.

Half Double Crochet (hdc)

How to half double crochet:

To begin a row of half double crochet, first stitch a foundation chain to the desired length. Add 2 extra chain stitches for the turning chain.

insert your hook into this stitch

Yarn over. With this yarn over, insert your hook into the third chain stitch from your hook. There will be 3 loops on your hook.

Yarn over again. Draw the yarn through the first loop only. There will still be 3 loops on your hook.

3

Yarn over and draw the yarn through all 3 loops on your hook.

4

You will have 1 loop on your hook when your first half double crochet stitch is complete.

5

insert your hook into this stitch

Yarn over. With this yarn over, insert your hook into the next chain stitch. There will be 3 loops on your hook. Repeat steps 2–4 to complete another half double crochet stitch.

6

Repeat step 5, working a half double crochet stitch into each chain stitch. At the end of the row, chain 2 for the turning chain.

7

insert your hook into this stitch

Turn your work so that the opposite side faces you. Yarn over and insert your hook into the second stitch. (The turning chain counts as the first half double crochet stitch in this row.) Repeat steps 2–4 to complete the stitch.

8

Repeat step 5 to continue making half double crochet stitches into each stitch of the previous row. At the end of this and all subsequent rows, chain 2 for the turning chain and turn.

Double Crochet (dc)

How to double crochet:

To begin a row of double crochet, first stitch a foundation chain to the desired length. Add 3 extra chain stitches for the turning chain.

1

insert your hook into this stitch

Yarn over. With this yarn over, insert your hook into the fourth chain stitch from your hook. There will be 3 loops on your hook.

2

Yarn over. Draw the yarn through the first loop on your hook. There will be 3 loops on your hook.

3

Yarn over. Draw the yarn through the first 2 loops on your hook only. There will now be 2 loops on your hook.

4

Yarn over again. Draw the yarn through the remaining 2 loops on your hook. You will have 1 loop on your hook when your first double crochet stitch is complete.

5

insert your hook into this stitch

Yarn over. Insert your hook into the next chain stitch. Repeat steps 2–4 to complete another double crochet stitch.

6

Repeat step 5, working a double crochet stitch into each chain stitch. At the end of the row, chain 3 for the turning chain. Turn your work so that the opposite side faces you.

7

insert your hook into this stitch

Yarn over and insert your hook into the second stitch. (The turning chain counts as the first double crochet stitch in this row.) Repeat steps 2–4 to complete the stitch.

8

Repeat step 5 to continue making double crochet stitches into each stitch of the previous row. At the end of this and all subsequent rows, chain 3 for the turning chain and turn.

Treble Crochet (tr)

How to treble crochet:

To begin a row of treble crochet, first stitch a foundation chain to the desired length. Add 4 extra chain stitches for the turning chain.

1

insert your hook into this stitch →

Yarn over twice. Insert your hook into the fifth chain stitch from your hook. There will be 4 loops on your hook.

2

Yarn over once. Draw the yarn through the first loop on your hook. There will be 4 loops on your hook.

3

Yarn over once. Draw the yarn through the first 2 loops on your hook. There will be 3 loops on your hook.

4

Yarn over once. Draw the yarn through the first 2 loops on your hook again. There will be 2 loops on your hook.

5

Yarn over. Draw the yarn through the remaining 2 loops on your hook. You will have 1 loop on your hook when your first treble crochet stitch is complete.

6

insert your hook into this stitch

Yarn over twice and insert your hook into the next chain stitch. Repeat steps 2–5 to complete another treble crochet stitch.

7

insert your hook into this stitch

Repeat step 6, working a treble crochet stitch into each chain. At the end of the row, chain 4 for the turning chain. Turn your work so that the opposite side faces you. Yarn over twice and insert your hook into the second stitch. Repeat steps 2–5 to complete the treble crochet stitch.

8

Repeat step 6 to continue making treble crochet stitches into each stitch of the previous row. At the end of this and all subsequent rows, chain 4 for the turning chain, yarn over twice, and insert your hook into the second stitch.

Decreasing Stitches (dec)

To decrease within a row, combine multiple stitches together.

Single Crochet Decrease

1 *insert your hook into this stitch*

Insert your hook into the next stitch as you would to start a single crochet.

2

Yarn over and draw the yarn through the stitch. There are now 2 loops on your hook.

3

Insert your hook into the next stitch. Yarn over and draw the yarn through the stitch. There are 3 loops on your hook.

4

Yarn over and draw the yarn through all 3 loops on your hook. You will have 1 loop on your hook when your first decrease is complete.

Double Crochet Decrease

1

Yarn over and insert your hook into the next stitch. Yarn over and draw the yarn through the stitch. Yarn over and draw the yarn through the first 2 loops. You will have 2 loops on your hook.

2

Yarn over and insert your hook into the next stitch. Yarn over and draw the yarn through the stitch. Yarn over and draw the yarn through the first 2 loops. You will have 3 loops on your hook.

3

Yarn over once. Draw the yarn through the first 2 loops on your hook. There will be 3 loops on your hook.

4

Yarn over once. Draw the yarn through the first 2 loops on your hook again. There will be 2 loops on your hook.

5

Yarn over. Draw the yarn through the remaining 2 loops on your hook. You will have 1 loop on your hook when your first treble crochet stitch is complete.

6

insert your hook into this stitch

Yarn over twice and insert your hook into the next chain stitch. Repeat steps 2–5 to complete another treble crochet stitch.

7

insert your hook into this stitch

Repeat step 6, working a treble crochet stitch into each chain. At the end of the row, chain 4 for the turning chain. Turn your work so that the opposite side faces you. Yarn over twice and insert your hook into the second stitch. Repeat steps 2–5 to complete the treble crochet stitch.

8

Repeat step 6 to continue making treble crochet stitches into each stitch of the previous row. At the end of this and all subsequent rows, chain 4 for the turning chain, yarn over twice, and insert your hook into the second stitch.

Decreasing Stitches (dec)

To decrease within a row, combine multiple stitches together.

Single Crochet Decrease

1 *insert your hook into this stitch*

Insert your hook into the next stitch as you would to start a single crochet.

2

Yarn over and draw the yarn through the stitch. There are now 2 loops on your hook.

3

Insert your hook into the next stitch. Yarn over and draw the yarn through the stitch. There are 3 loops on your hook.

4

Yarn over and draw the yarn through all 3 loops on your hook. You will have 1 loop on your hook when your first decrease is complete.

Double Crochet Decrease

1

Yarn over and insert your hook into the next stitch. Yarn over and draw the yarn through the stitch. Yarn over and draw the yarn through the first 2 loops. You will have 2 loops on your hook.

2

Yarn over and insert your hook into the next stitch. Yarn over and draw the yarn through the stitch. Yarn over and draw the yarn through the first 2 loops. You will have 3 loops on your hook.

3

Yarn over and draw the yarn through all 3 loops on your hook. You will have 1 loop on your hook when your first decrease is complete.

Increasing Stitches (inc)

To increase within a row, work multiple stitches into the same stitch.

Single Crochet Increase

1

Insert your hook back into the same stitch you did your last single crochet in. Work another single crochet into that same stitch.

2

You will have 1 loop on your hook when your first single crochet increase is complete.

Double Crochet Increase

1

Insert your hook back into the same stitch in the previous row. Work another double crochet into that same stitch.

2

You will have 1 loop on your hook when your first double crochet increase is complete.

Front & Back Loops (FL & BL)

Working into the front or back loop only will create a unique texture and line.
These examples use half double crochet, but you can use these techniques with other stitches.

Tip: When your crochet work is in front of you, the front loop is the loop closer to you, while the back loop is farther from you.

front loop   back loop

Front Loops

1

To work a half double crochet stitch into the front loop, yarn over and insert your hook into only the front loop facing you. Complete the stitch as usual.

2

Continue working half double crochet stitches into only the front loops of the stitches in the previous row until you reach the end of the row. This creates a line.

Back Loops

1

To work a half double crochet stitch into the back loop, yarn over and insert your hook into only the back loop facing away from you. Complete the stitch as usual.

2

Continue working half double crochet stitches into only the back loops of the stitches in the previous row until you reach the end of the row. This creates another line.

Working into Spaces

Some patterns will ask you to work into a space rather than a stitch of a previous row or round. This technique is demonstrated below using double crochet.

1

Start at the position where you want to work into a space. Yarn over.

2

Insert your hook from front to back into the space (instead of the stitch). Yarn over and pull the yarn through the space.

3

Finish your double crochet as usual. You will have 1 loop on your hook when your first double crochet stitch into the space is complete.

Here is the row finished with double crochet stitches worked into the spaces.

Tip: Working into spaces is often called for when starting a round and in many floral motifs. In the example to the right, multiple stitches have been made into the spaces.

Working in Rounds

To begin working in rounds, you have to first start with a center ring. There are 2 different methods for starting a round, with a chain stitch ring or a magic circle.

Chain Stitch Ring

The chain stitch ring is made up of chain stitches that are joined together to form a ring. This method leaves a small opening in the center of your round.

Tip: Patterns will tell you how many chains to start with and what stitches to use. This example uses single crochet.

1 Chain 5 for a foundation chain. Insert your hook back into the first chain you made.

2 Work a slip stitch into that chain to form a ring.

3 Insert your hook into the center of the ring. Work a single crochet stitch into the ring.

4 Continue working single crochet stitches into the ring until you have made the required number of stitches. (For this example, 6 single crochet stitches.)

5

Work a slip stitch into the first single crochet you made to close up the ring.

6

You are now ready to start a round. (See page 31.)

Magic Circle

The magic circle forms a ring with your yarn that your first round of stitches are attached to. The ends are pulled to leave no opening in the center. That's the magic!

Tip: A chain stitch ring can replace a magic circle in a pattern.

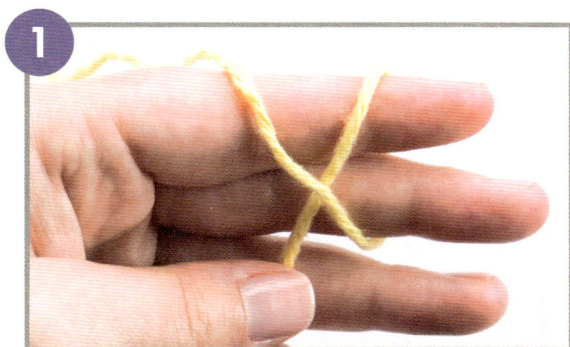

1

Loop the yarn around your fingers as shown to form an X.

2

Take your hook under the bottom strand of the X. Use your hook to draw the other strand under the bottom strand. It will form a loose loop on your hook.

3

Remove the circle of yarn from your fingers. Yarn over. Draw the yarn through the loop on your hook. (This does not count as your first single crochet stitch.)

4

You should now have a circle with the tail and the working yarn on the left side.

5

Insert your hook into the center of the circle. You are going to work a single crochet into that space. Yarn over and draw the yarn through the circle and tail. You will have 2 loops on your hook.

6

Yarn over again and draw the yarn through the remaining 2 loops on your hook. You will have 1 loop on your hook when your first single crochet stitch into the circle is complete.

7

Continue working the required number of single crochet stitches into the circle, making sure you are always working around the circle and the tail. If you run out of tail, pull it slightly. This closes the circle a little, but allows you to have a longer tail to work around.

8

When you have worked 6 single crochet stitches into the circle, pull the tail tightly to close the circle.

9

Insert your hook into the first single crochet stitch you made and make a slip stitch to close the circle.

10

With your slip stitch complete, you are now ready to start a round.

Starting a Round

To start a round, first begin by using either the chain stitch ring or magic circle method. This example used the magic circle method.

Round 1:

1

insert your hook under these 2 loops

Chain 1. Insert your hook under the top 2 loops of the first stitch and work a single crochet into that stitch.

2

Work 2 single crochets into each of the remaining stitches. (You will have 12 stitches.) Insert your hook back into the first stitch and make a slip stitch to close the round.

Rounds 2–6:

Each round increases by 6 stitches. The increases are evenly spaced in order to keep the circular shape. Close each round with a slip stitch back into the first stitch and then chain 1.

Round 2: Single crochet an increase in every other stitch for a total of 18 stitches.
Round 3: Single crochet an increase in every third stitch for a total of 24 stitches.
Round 4: Single crochet an increase in every fourth stitch for a total of 30 stitches.
Round 5: Single crochet an increase in every fifth stitch for a total of 36 stitches.
Round 6: Single crochet an increase in every sixth stitch for a total of 42 stitches.

For additional rounds, continue to evenly increase your rounds by 6 until your desired circumference.

Joining in New Yarn

At the End of a Row

1

To join in new yarn at the end of a row, work the last stitch with the old yarn until the final yarn over of the stitch. Yarn over with the new yarn.

2

Draw the new yarn through both loops on your hook. There is 1 loop on your hook. Continue stitching with the new yarn as usual.

In the Middle of a Row

1

To join in new yarn in the middle of a row, work the last stitch with the old yarn until the final yarn over of the stitch. Yarn over with the new yarn.

2

Draw the new yarn through both loops on your hook. There is 1 loop on your hook. Continue stitching with the new yarn as usual until you reach the end of the row.

Tip: Rather than leaving the tail of the old yarn in the middle of the row, you can work over the old yarn until you reach the end of the row. You can then weave in all yarn tails at the edges later.

Fastening Off

1

After completing your last stitch, cut the excess yarn, leaving several inches to weave the tail in later. Yarn over and draw the yarn tail through the loop on your hook.

2

Pull the yarn tail to tighten.

Weaving in the Tail

1

Thread one of your yarn tails into a blunt-tipped needle. Insert the needle into the first stitch and draw the yarn through.

2

Continue weaving the needle under and over the stitches around the edge.

3

Cut the yarn close to the final stitch when you're done weaving in the tail.

Crochet Gift Patterns

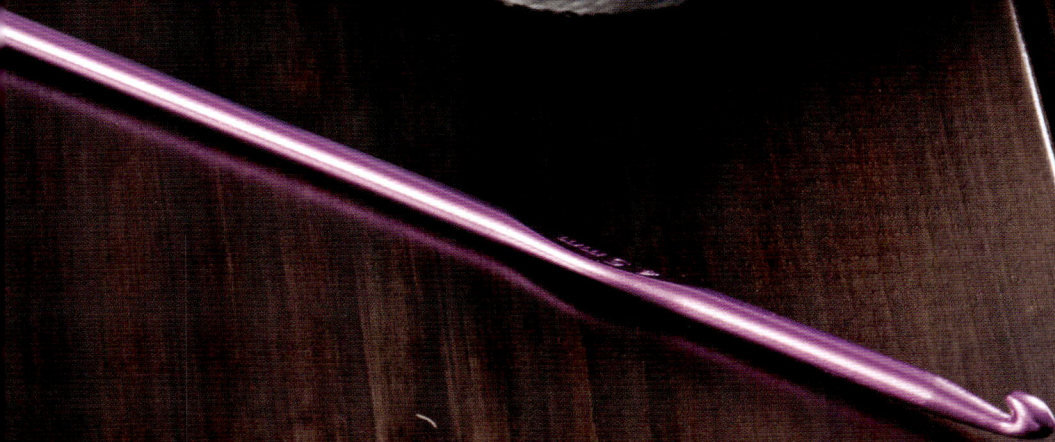

Bracelet

Skill Level

■□□□
BEGINNER

Materials

MEDIUM 4

Hook: 4.5 mm/U.S. 7
Other: Yarn needle

Stitches Used

Chain stitch (ch)
Double crochet (dc)

Instructions

Ch 108 (or to desired length depending on wrist size).

Row 1: Dc in 3rd ch from hook and in each ch across row. Fasten off, leaving a long tail for sewing the bracelet together.

Tip: This chunky bracelet makes a great addition to any outfit.

Assembly

1. Fold into thirds.
2. Braid the three sections together to your liking.
3. Once braided, fold the bracelet in half.
4. With the long tail and a yarn needle, sew the ends of the bracelet together evenly.
5. Fasten off and weave in ends.

Tip: To use a different yarn weight, adjust the number of chain stitches depending on the thickness of the yarn.

Elephant

Skill Level

EASY

Materials

MEDIUM 4 1 skein

Hook: 4 mm/U.S. G-6

Other: Polyfill stuffing, safety eyes, stitch marker, yarn needle

Stitches Used

Chain stitch (ch)

Half double crochet (hdc)

Magic circle

Single crochet (sc)

Single crochet 2 together (sc2tog)

Slip stitch (sl st)

Instructions

Body

Make a magic circle.

Round 1: Work 6 sc into magic circle. Place stitch marker to indicate beg of rnd, and move marker up as each rnd is completed.

Round 2: 2 sc in each st around.

Round 3: *2 sc in next st, sc in next st; rep from * around.

Round 4: *2 sc in next st, sc in next 2 sts; rep from * around.

Round 5: *2 sc in next st, sc in next 3 sts; rep from * around.

Round 6: *2 sc in next st, sc in next 4 sts; rep from * around.

Round 7: *2 sc in next st, sc in next 5 sts; rep from * around.

Rounds 8–17: Sc in each st around.

Round 18: *Sc2tog, sc in next 5 sts; rep from * around.

Round 19: *Sc2tog, sc in next 4 sts; rep from * around.

Round 20: *Sc2tog, sc in next 3 sts; rep from * around.

Attach safety eyes and stuff elephant body. If using buttons for eyes, wait until entire elephant is done to sew on eyes.

Trunk

Cont working in rnds from body. Stuff trunk as you work and shape trunk how you want it to hang.

Round 1: Sc in each st around.

Round 2: *Sc2tog, sc in next 4 sts; rep from * around.

Rounds 3–4: Sc in each st around.

Round 5: *Sc2tog, sc in next 3 sts; rep from * around.

Rounds 6–7: Sc in each st around.

Round 8: *Sc2tog, sc in next 2 sts; rep from * around.

Round 9: Sc in each st around.

Round 10: *Sc2tog, sc in next st; rep from * around. Fasten off and weave in ends.

Ears (make 2)

Ch 7 for the foundation chain.

Row 1: Starting from 2nd ch from hook, sc 5 in back loops of foundation chain. 3 sc in last st. Turn the chain, sc 4 in front loops of foundation chain, then 2 sc in next front loop. (This will make an oval shape.)

Row 2: 2 sc in next st, sc in next 4 sts, [2 sc in next st] 3 times, sc in next 4 sts, [2 sc in next st] 2 times.

Row 3: Sc, 2 sc in next st, sc in next 5 sts, 2 sc in next st, sc, 2 sc in next st, sc, 2 sc in next st, sc in next 5 sts, 2 sc in next st, sc, 2 sc in next st.

Row 4: Sc, 2 sc in next st, sc in next 8 sts, 2 sc in next st, sc, 2 sc in next st, sc, 2 sc in next st, sc in next 8 sts, 2 sc in next st, sc, 2 sc in next st.

Fasten off, leaving long tail for sewing. Fold crocheted piece in half so it curves inward, sew ears to body using long tail and weave in.

Legs (make 4)

Make a magic circle.

Round 1: Work 6 sc into magic circle. Place stitch marker to indicate beg of rnd, and move marker up as each rnd is completed.

Round 2: 2 sc in each st around.

Rounds 3–5: Sc in each st around. Fasten off, leaving a long tail for sewing. Stuff and sew onto body using the long tail and weave in.

Tail

Join yarn with a sl st at the back of elephant body and ch 5. Work 3 hdc in 2nd ch from hook. Fasten off.

Tip: This adorable elephant is the perfect addition to a baby's nursery. Crochet one elephant or an entire herd.

Snowflakes

Hook: 4.5 mm/U.S. 7
Other: Decoupage glue, foam brush (optional)

Stitches Used

Chain stitch (ch)

Cluster

Half double crochet (hdc)

Magic circle

Slip stitch (sl st)

Skill Level

◖◻◻◻
BEGINNER

Materials

MEDIUM
4

Instructions

Round 1: Make a magic circle and ch 4 (this counts as hdc, ch 2), *hdc, ch 2; rep from * 5 times into the magic circle. Sl st in top of ch 4 to close round.

Round 2: Working into the 6 spaces you created, make clusters as follows: *sl st in first sp, ch 3, sl st into same sp, ch 5, sl st into same sp, ch 3, sl st into same sp *; rep from * to * 5 more times, then sl st into the very first sl st, fasten off, and weave in ends.

Finishing (optional)

With a foam brush, apply decoupage glue to stiffen snowflake. Add glitter to the glue for extra sparkle.

Tip: Dress up a wrapped gift by topping it with a crocheted snowflake rather than a bow.

Drink Sleeve

Skill Level

■■□□ EASY

Materials

MEDIUM 4 (in 2 colors)

Hook: 5 mm/U.S. H-8
Other: Stitch marker, yarn needle

Stitches Used

Chain stitch (ch)
Double crochet (dc)
Half double crochet (hdc)
Magic circle
Single crochet (sc)
Slip stitch (sl st)
Treble crochet (tr)

Instructions

Drink sleeve

Ch 28 (or enough to just fit around the cup). Do not join.

Row 1: Sc in 2nd ch from hook and in each st across row. Fold in half and join with sl st to first sc to create a continuous round.

Round 2: Ch 1, sc in same st as join, sc in each st around.

Rounds 3–11: Ch 1, sc in same st and each st around. (For a taller sleeve, just keep going!)

Round 12: Sl st around, fasten off, and weave in ends.

Heart pocket

Make a magic circle.

Round 1: *All into the magic circle:* 3 tr (place stitch marker in the first tr), 3 dc, ch 1, 1 tr, ch 1, 3 dc, 3 tr. Ch 3, sl st back into the circle.

Round 2: Ch 3, sc and hdc in first tr, 3 hdc in next st, 2 hdc in next st, sc in next four sts, ch 1, dc in tr, ch 1, sc in next four sts, 2 hdc in next st, 3 hdc in next st, hdc and sc in next st, (tighten loop as much as possible here) ch 3 and sl st in center. Fasten off, leaving a long tail for sewing. Weave in ends.

Finishing

Weave the yarn tail under a few sts so you are beginning to sew at the end of one of the heart's top arches. Position heart on front of sleeve, covering the visible seam. Stitch heart to sleeve, leaving top of the heart open and unattached.

Tip: Add a coffee shop gift card and a "Thanks a Latte" note for the coffee lover in your life.

Mittens

Hook: 4 mm/U.S. G-6
Other: Yarn needle

Skill Level

■■□□
EXPERIENCED

Materials

MEDIUM
4 2 skeins

Stitches Used

Chain stitch (ch)
Single crochet (sc)
Single crochet 2 together (sc2tog)
Slip stitch (sl st)

Tip: The back bump

The back bump is the back side of a chain stitch. The front of a chain stitch has the two loops that form the V that you would normally insert your hook under. The back bump is on the opposite side of a chain stitch. If you turn the chain upside down, so that you're looking at the bottom of it, you'll see a line of ridges. You would insert your hook under each ridge if instructed to crochet into the back bump of each chain stitch.

Instructions

Ribbing

Row 1: Ch 11, 1 sc st into the back bump of the 2nd ch from hook, make 1 sc st into the remaining sts.

Row 2: Ch 1, turn, 1 sc through back loop into each st across.

Rows 3–34: Rep row 2.

Fold ribbing in half and line up short edges. Sl st these rows together by inserting your hook into the back loop of the foundation chain and then through the back loop of the stitch directly behind it (from the last row worked). Do not fasten off! Turn ribbing tube so that the sl st row is on the inside. You will now stitch into the edges of previous rows.

Body of each mitten

Round 1: Make 34 sc sts, equally spaced, around top edge of ribbing.

Round 2: 1 sc into each of the next 15 sts, 2 sc into the next st, 1 sc into each of the next 2 sts, 2 sc into the next st, 1 sc into each of the next 14 sts.

Round 3: 1 sc into each st around.

Round 4: 1 sc into each of the next 16 sts, 2 sc into the next st, 1 sc into each of the next 2 sts, 2 sc into the next st, 1 sc into each of the next 15 sts.

Round 5: 1 sc into each st around.

Round 6: 1 sc into each of the next 17 sts, 2 sc into the next st, 1 sc into each of the next 2 sts, 2 sc into the next st, 1 sc into each of the next 16 sts.

Round 7: 1 sc into each st around.

Round 8: 1 sc into each of the next 18 sts, 2 sc into the next st, 1 sc into each of the next 2 sts, 2 sc into the next st, 1 sc into each of the next 17 sts.

Round 9: 1 sc into each st around.

Round 10: 1 sc into each of the next 19 sts, 2 sc into the next st, 1 sc into each of the next 2 sts, 2 sc into the next st, 1 sc into each of the next 18 sts.

Round 11: 1 sc into each st around.

Round 12: 1 sc into each of the next 20 sts, 2 sc into the next st, 1 sc into each of the next 2 sts, 2 sc into the next st, 1 sc into each of the next 19 sts.

Round 13: 1 sc into each st around.

Round 14: 1 sc into each of the next 21 sts, 2 sc into the next st, 1 sc into each of the next 2 sts, 2 sc into the next st, 1 sc into each of the next 20 sts.

Round 15: 1 sc into each st around.

Round 16: 1 sc into each of the next 17 sts, sk the next 14 sts (for thumb), 1 sc into each of the next 16 sts.

Round 17: 1 sc into each st around.

Rep round 17 until the measurement from the thumbhole up is 3.5" (approx 15 more rounds).

Next round: [1 sc into each of the next 9 sts, sc2tog] 3 times.

Next round: 1 sc in each st around.

Next round: [1 sc into each of the next 3 sts, sc2tog] 6 times.

Next round: 1 sc into each st around.

Next round: Sc2tog 12 times.

Next round: 1 sc into each st around.

Next round: [1 sc into the next st, sc2tog] 4 times. Fasten off with a 10" tail. Using yarn needle, thread yarn tail through the front loop of the remaining 8 sts and pull tight. Weave in ends.

Thumb

Join yarn to any thumb st and sc 14 stitches around.

Continue working in rounds with 1 sc into each st until thumb measures 2.5" from nook (approx 9 more rounds).

Next round: Sc2tog 7 times and fasten off with a 10" tail. Using yarn needle, thread yarn tail through the front loop of the remaining 7 sts and pull tight. Weave in ends.

One mitten done and one to go!

Tip: These comfy mittens are great for keeping hands warm. Crochet a matching hat (see page 64) for a gift set.

Flower Hair Pin

Tip: Use a smaller hook to create a smaller flower.

Instructions

Make a magic circle.

Round 1: Work 16 sc into circle.

Round 2: In first sc, work *[1 sc, ch 3, 1 sc], sk next st; rep from * 7 more times, join with sl st in first sc of round (you should have 8 ch-3 sps).

Round 3: Work 5 sc in each ch-3 sp around, join with sl st in first sc of round. Fasten off and weave in ends.

Finishing

Add a dab of glue to the flower and attach to hair pin. For a firmer flower, apply decoupage glue to stiffen yarn.

Tip: Crocheted flowers are the perfect addition to any accessory. Try stringing multiple flowers together to make a crocheted necklace or garland.

Wine Carrier

Other: Stitch marker, yarn needle

Stitches Used

Chain stitch (ch)
Half double crochet (hdc)
Magic circle
Single crochet (sc)
Slip stitch (sl st)
Spike half double crochet (spike hdc)
Spike single crochet (spike sc)

Skill Level

EASY

Materials

 BULKY **5** 2 skeins

Hook: 5 mm/U.S. H-8

Instructions

Base

Make a magic circle.

Round 1: Sc 6 times into the circle. Place stitch marker to indicate beg of rnd, and move marker up as each rnd is completed.

Round 2: Sc twice into each st around.

Round 3: *Sc twice into next st, sc once into the next st; rep from * around.

Round 4: *Sc twice into the next st, sc once into the next 2 sts; rep from * around.

Round 5: *Sc twice into the next st, sc once into the next 3 sts; rep from * around.

Round 6: *Sc twice into the next st, sc once into the next 4 sts; rep from * around.

Round 7: Sc once into the back loop only on each st around.

Round 8: Sc in each st around.

Round 9: Spike sc into the next st, *sc into the next st, spike sc into the next st; rep from * around.

Round 10: Sc into the next st, *spike sc into the next st, sc into the next st; rep from * around.

Rounds 11–14: Repeat rounds 9 and 10.

Round 15: *Spike hdc into the next st, hdc into the next st; rep from * around.

Round 16: Hdc in each st around.

Round 17: Sc in each st around.

Tip: A bottle of wine makes a nice gift, but presenting it in a crocheted wine carrier makes a nice gift unforgettable.

Rounds 18–23: Repeat rounds 9 and 10.

Rounds 24–26: Repeat rounds 15–17.

Rounds 27–32: Repeat rounds 9 and 10.

Rounds 33–35: Repeat rounds 15–17.

Rounds 36–41: Repeat rounds 9 and 10.

Rounds 42–44: Repeat rounds 15–17.

Tip: **How to make the spike hdc**
Make your half double crochet in the stitch in the round below the round you are working on.

Handles

Round 45: Repeat round 9.

Round 46: Sc 4, ch 11, sk 9 sts, sc 8, ch 11, sk 9 sts, sc 4.

Rounds 47–48: Sc in each st around.

Round 49: *Spike sc in next st, sc in next st; rep from * around, sl st in first st of round to secure, fasten off and weave in ends.

Finishing

Close the magic circle tightly and weave in all ends.

Tip: **How to make the spike sc**
Make your single crochet in the stitch in the round below the round you are working on.

Fleece Blanket Edges

Skill Level

BEGINNER

Materials

MEDIUM 4

Hook: 5 mm/U.S. H-8
Other: ½ yard of fleece, crochet edge fleece blade, cutting mat, yarn needle

Stitches Used

Chain stitch (ch)
Double crochet (dc)
Half double crochet (hdc)
Slip stitch (sl st)

Instructions

Place piece of fleece on top of cutting mat. About a half-inch from the edge of fleece, go around entire blanket with the crochet edge fleece blade. As the blade wheel turns, it creates perfectly spaced little holes for crochet stitches around blanket. Put your hook through a corner hole. Attach yarn.

Round 1: *Hdc, ch 1; rep from * in each hole around fleece, placing 2 (hdc, ch 1) in each corner.

Round 2 (border pattern): *3 dc in ch-1 sp, 3 dc in next ch-1 sp, sl st in next ch-1 sp; rep from * around fleece, placing 3 (3 dc in ch-1 sp) in each corner.

Fasten off and weave in ends.

Tip: Make sure your piece of fleece is cut evenly into a square or rectangle before starting.

Mason Jar Cozy

Skill Level

■■□□ **EASY**

Materials

MEDIUM 4

Hook: 3.5 mm/U.S. E-4

Other: Mason jar (any size), yarn needle

Stitches Used

Chain stitch (ch)
Double crochet (dc)
Single crochet (sc)
Slip stitch (sl st)

Instructions

Chain in multiples of 6, measuring around the circumference of your Mason jar as you go, until you have the right length. Err on the side of slightly too tight versus too loose, as the yarn will stretch a little and you want a tight fit. Join with a sl st into the first ch to form a ring.

Round 1: Ch 3 (counts as first dc), dc into each st around, join with a sl st to top of initial ch 3.

Round 2: Ch 1, sc into first dc (ch 3 from previous round), sc into next 2 sts, *ch 3, skip next 3 sts, sc into next 3 sts; rep from * around, join with a sl st to first sc.

Round 3: Sl st into next st (should be the middle of the 3 sc from previous round), ch 1, 5 dc into ch-3 sp, *skip next st, 1 sc into next st, skip next st, 5 dc into next ch-3 sp; rep from * around, join with a sl st into first ch 1.

Round 4: Sl st into next 2 sts, ch 1, sc into same st, sc into next 2 sts (there should now be a sc in the middle 3 of the 5 dc sts from the previous round), *ch 3, skip next 3 sts (1 dc, 1 sc, 1 dc skipped from previous round), sc into next 3 sts; rep from * around, join with a sl st to top of first sc.

Round 5: Sl st across to the middle st of the 3 sc from previous round, ch 1, 5 dc into ch-3 sp, *skip 1 st, 1 sc into next st (middle sc of previous 3), 5 dc into ch-3 sp; rep from * around, join with a sl st into first ch 1.

Repeat rounds 4 and 5 until you have the correct height for your jar. Fasten off and weave in ends.

Tip: This cozy was made to fit a regular mouth 1 pint (16 oz.) Mason jar. The completed cozy is about 3.5" high with a circumference of about 11".

Slippers

Other: Stitch marker, yarn needle

Stitches Used

Chain stitch (ch)
Double crochet (dc)
Double crochet 2 together (dc2tog)
Double crochet 3 together (dc3tog)
Single crochet (sc)
Slip stitch (sl st)

Skill Level

INTERMEDIATE

Materials

MEDIUM 4 — 2 skeins (1 of each color)

Hook: 4.5 mm/U.S. 7

Instructions

Pattern is worked from heel to toe.

Slippers (make 2)

With main color, ch 18, leaving a long tail.

Row 1: Dc in fourth ch from hook, dc in next 5 ch sts, 2 dc in each of next 2 ch sts, dc in each st to end of row. Ch 3, turn.

Row 2: Sk first dc, dc in next 7 sts, 2 dc in each of next 2 sts, dc in each st to end of row. Ch 3, turn.

Row 3: Sk first dc, dc in next 8 sts, 2 dc in each of next 2 sts, dc in each st to end of row. Ch 3, turn.

Row 4: Sk first dc, dc in each st across to end of row. Ch 3, turn.

Row 5: Sk first dc, dc2tog, dc in each st to last 3 sts, dc2tog, dc in last st (last st is the ch 3 of prev row). Ch 3, turn.

Row 6: Sk first dc, dc in each st across row. Ch 3, turn.

Rows 7–12: Rep row 6.

Row 13: Dc in first st (top of turning ch 3), 2 dc in next st, dc in each st to last 2 sts, 2 dc in each of the last 2 sts. Ch 3, turn.

Rows 14–15: Rep row 13.

Row 16: Dc in first st (top of turning ch 3), 2 dc in next st, dc in next 8 sts, dc2tog 6 times, dc in next 8 sts, 2 dc in each of the rem 2 sts. Ch 3, turn.

Row 17: Dc in first st (top of turning ch 3), 2 dc in next st, dc in next 6 sts, dc2tog 7 times, dc in next 6 sts, 2 dc in each of the last 2 sts. Ch 3, turn.

Row 18: Sk first dc, dc in next 7 sts, dc2tog twice, dc3tog, dc2tog twice, dc in last 8 sts. FO, leaving a long tail. Use the beg tail to seam up the back edge to form the heel of slipper.

Assembly

Assembly is different for each slipper. The folds at the toe vary depending on the right or left slipper.

Tip: To make a smaller size, crochet fewer rows from 7–12 (the sole) and make a few sc decreases when you work the border. To make a larger size, just add rows from 7–12.

Finishing left slipper

1. Place a stitch marker into beg ch 3 of row 16.

2. Leaving a long tail, attach the border color yarn at end of row 18 with right side of row 18 facing.

3. Sc down side of last 4 rows, making 2 sc into each row.

4. Folding the opposite flap down into slipper, make the next sc into 5th row and also the ch-3 with a marker in it. Make next sc into the next st only in the 5th row. Cont making 2 sc into the side of the rows.

5. When you get to the heel, make only 1 sc into row, then skip the heel seam and make 1 sc in first row. Make 2 sc in the rows back up toward the toe.

6. When you get to the joining sc, sl st into it, then sl st into all sc you just made around the slipper opening.

7. FO and weave in that end. Seam the toe sts down so the seam lines up with where the edge of your toes will be. Weave in ends.

Finishing right slipper

1. Place a stitch marker into beg ch 3 of row 16.

2. Flip slipper inside out so the row 18 tail is now on the opposite side.

3. Leaving a long tail, attach the border color yarn at row 15, with the right side of row 15 facing you. 2 sc into the side of that dc. 2 sc into side of each row of dc toward the heel. Make only 1 sc into the rows at the seam and then 2 sc into the side of each row of dc back toward the toe.

4. When you reach the 5th row from top, make 1 sc into that row, then make 1 sc into the same row and also the beg ch-3 of row 16 (directly to the right of the first sc).

5. Cont making 2 sc into the sides of rem 4 dc rows. FO, leaving a long tail.

6. Attach border color yarn at joining sc. Sl st into 1 sc of prev row. Sl st around slipper opening. FO and weave in that end. Seam the edges down so the seam lines up where the edge of your toes will be. Weave in ends.

Bath Pouf

Skill Level

■ □ □ □
BEGINNER

Materials

BULKY 5

Hook: 5 mm/U.S. H-8
Other: Yarn needle

Stitches Used

Chain stitch (ch)
Double crochet (dc)
Single crochet (sc)
Slip stitch (sl st)

Instructions

Ch 5, join with a sl st in first ch to form ring.

Ch 35 and sl st into ring. (This makes the cord with which to hang up the bath pouf.)

Round 1: Ch 1, 25 sc into ring. Sl st in first sc to join.

Round 2: Ch 2, 3 dc in each st around. Join with a sl st to top of first dc.

Rounds 3–4: Rep round 2.

Fasten off and weave in ends.

Tip: When choosing yarn, keep in mind that 100% cotton yarn will make the bath pouf very dense when wet, so it's best to have some nylon in the yarn. The yarn used for this bath pouf was 54% cotton, 24% linen, and 22% nylon.

Crochet Clutch

Skill Level

■■■▢
INTERMEDIATE

Materials

MEDIUM 4 2 skeins (1 of each color)

Hook: 5 mm/H-8
Other: Stitch marker, yarn needle

Stitches Used

Chain stitch (ch)

Cluster

Double crochet (dc)

Half double crochet (hdc)

Single crochet (sc)

Slip stitch (sl st)

Instructions

Ch 33. Place stitch marker in the first st of each round, and move marker up as each round is completed.

Round 1: Work 2 sc in second ch from hook. Sc in each st until last ch st, 3 sc in last st. Cont working across the other side of chain with a sc in each st until end.

Round 2: Work 2 sc in each of the next 2 sts, sc across until the 3 turning sts of the round, 2 sc in each of those 3 sts and cont sc across until last st. 2 sc in last st.

Round 3: Work 1 sc in each st around.

Round 4: Rep round 3.

Round 5: Work (sc, 2 dc) in next st, *sk 2 sts, work (sc, 2 dc) in next st; rep from * until the last 2 sts. Sk 2 sts, sl st to first sc to join.

Round 6: Ch 1, turn. Work (sc, 2 dc) into same st as join. *Sk 2 dc, work (sc, 2 dc) in next sc; rep from * until the last 2 sts. Sk 2 dc, sl st to first sc to join.

Rounds 7–14: Rep round 6.

Round 15: Ch 1, turn. Sk first sc, work 1 sc into each of the next 36 sts. *Sk 2 dc, work (sc, 2 dc) in next sc; rep from * until last 2 sts. Sk 2 dc, work 1 sc in joining st.

Pattern will now continue as the flap of the clutch and will be worked in rows. Each row will be only half of the diameter of the clutch.

Row 16: Ch 1 (counts as first sc), turn. Work 2 dc in first sc. *Sk 2 dc, work (sc, 2 dc) in next sc; rep from * until end of row. Sk 2 dc, work 1 sc in last sc.

Row 17: Ch 1 (counts as first sc), turn. Work 2 dc in first sc. *Sk 2 dc, work (sc, 2 dc) in next sc; rep from * until end of row. Sk 2 dc, 1 sc in turning ch at end of row.

Rows 18–24: Rep row 17.

Finishing

Join in new color. Ch 1, turn. Sk first st, work (sc, hdc, sc) in next st. *Sk next st, work (sc, hdc, sc) in next st; rep from * across to last dc. Sk last dc, work 5 (sc, hdc, sc) clusters evenly spaced across the side of the flap. Sk first sc, work (sc, hdc, sc) in next st. *Sk next st, work (sc, hdc, sc) in next st; rep from * across. Work 5 (sc, hdc, sc) clusters evenly spaced across the other side of the flap. Sl st to first sc to join. Fasten off and weave in ends.

Tip: This crochet clutch makes a great gift. Stitch it in the recipient's favorite colors.

Ornament

Hook: 4.5 mm/U.S. 7
Other: Yarn needle

Skill Level

EASY

Materials

MEDIUM
4

Stitches Used

Chain stitch (ch)
Double crochet (dc)
Magic circle
Slip stitch (sl st)

Instructions

Each ornament is made from 6 discs that are slip stitched together as you go. Change colors each time you start a new disc.

Disc 1

Make a magic circle.

Round 1: Ch 2 (counts as dc here and throughout), 11 dc into circle, pull circle closed, join with a sl st into the starting ch.

Round 2: Ch 2, dc into same st, 2 dc into each st around, join with a sl st.

Round 3: Ch 2, dc into next st, ch 1, *dc into each of next 2 sts, ch 1; rep from * around, join with a sl st. Fasten off, leaving a long tail (this will be used later to make the hanging loop). Do not weave in ends.

Disc 2

Chain 12, join with a sl st to form ring.

Round 1: Ch 2, 23 dc into ring, join with a sl st.

Round 2: Ch 2, dc into next st. Place disc 1 in front of disc 2 and sl st through the ch-sp on disc 1 (the space before the final ch-sp). Dc into each of next 2 sts on disc 2, ch 1, *dc into next 2 sts, sk 1 ch-sp on disc 1 and sl st into the next ch-sp, dc into each of next 2 sts on disc 2, ch 1; rep from * around, join with a sl st. (Disc 2 is joined to disc 1 by 6 sl sts in alternating ch-sps. The 6 ch-sps on disc 2 will be used to attach disc 3 in the same way.) Pull tail from center of disc 1 through hole in disc 2.

Discs 3–5

Rep disc 2, but work the sl sts into the empty ch-sps of previous disc.

Tip: This crocheted ornament makes a great gift for anyone on your list. Crochet one ornament or make a set.

Disc 6

Rounds 1–2: Rep rounds 1 and 2 of disc 1. Take the tail from disc 1, which is pulled through the middle of all the other discs, and tightly tie it together with the tail of disc 6 so that the centers of disc 1 and 6 are fastened together through the other discs.

Round 3: Rep round 2 of disc 2. Fasten off, leaving a tail for sewing.

Finishing

Thread tail from disc 6 into yarn needle and pass through each of the ch-sps from the inside out for each one, and for the starting ch-sp. Pull yarn tight to draw the ch-sps together, and weave in end.

Rep on other side, using long tail from round 3 of disc 1 to make hanging loop before fastening off.

Tablet Pouch

Hook: 9 mm/U.S. M-13
Other: Yarn needle

Skill Level

■■■□ INTERMEDIATE

Materials

BULKY 5 — 2 skeins (1 of each color)

Stitches Used

Chain stitch (ch)
Single crochet (sc)

Tip: This pouch is about 8.5" wide and 10" high with the flap closed.

Tip: If you want the same number of peaks, but a different width for your pouch, add or remove foundation chains from each peak in multiples of 5.

Instructions

This tablet pouch is made from a vertical strip that will be folded in half with an extra length as the flap.

With first color, ch 31, turn.

Row 1: Sk first st, sc in next 6 sts, 3 sc in next st, sc in next 6 sts. Sk next 2 sts, sc in next 6 sts, 3 sc in next st, sc in next 6 sts. Sk 1 st, sc in last st. Ch 1, turn.

Rows 2–4: Rep row 1.

Change color.

Rows 5–8: Rep row 1.

Continue repeating row 1, changing colors every 4 rows until desired size. Fasten off and weave in ends. (The pouch will fold up vertically, leaving an extra extension for the fold-over flap, so you will need more than twice your tablet's height.)

Once desired size is reached, fold vertically, leaving extension for fold-over flap. Using color you want for edges, attach yarn at bottom corner of pouch. Sc evenly through both side edges up until where the fold-over flap will begin. Once sides are seamed together, continue working sc sts around the edges of the fold-over flap. Fasten off and weave in ends.

Attach same color yarn for edges on the opposite side and repeat process. Fasten off and weave in ends when done.

Baby Bib

Skill Level

■ ■ □ □ □
EASY

Materials

MEDIUM 4 2 skeins (1 of each color)

Hook: 4.5 mm/U.S. 7
Other: 1 button,
yarn needle

Stitches Used

Chain stitch (ch)
Double crochet (dc)
Single crochet (sc)

Instructions

With main color, ch 35 (or until chain is approx 7" long).

Row 1: Ch 2, *dc, sc*; rep from * to * in each ch across to end of row.

Row 2: Ch 2, turn. *Sc, dc*; rep from * to * in each st across to end of row. (The single crochets should be in the double crochets below, and the double crochets should be in the single crochets below.)

Rows 3 and on: Rep rows 1–2 until bib measures approx 6.5" or to desired length.

Strap

Next row: Ch 2, turn. Depending on where you ended in prev row, either *sc, dc* or *dc, sc* until row is approx 1" wide.

Next row: Ch 2, turn. Either *sc, dc* or *dc, sc*, repeating from * to * across to end of row.

Next row: Cont alternating between either a *sc, dc* or *dc, sc* row until strap measures approx 8.5" or to desired length.

Buttonhole row: Rep prev row, but, once reaching the center two sts, ch 2 and sk the center two sts.

Final 2 rows: Ch 2, turn. Sc in each st across. Fasten off and weave in ends.

Border

Change colors. Attach yarn anywhere, and sc in each st around bib, placing the single crochets evenly along edges of bib. Fasten off and weave in ends.

Button

Using a threaded yarn needle, sew button on the opposite side of strap. Weave in ends securely.

Men's Hat

Skill Level

BEGINNER

Materials

SUPER BULKY 6 2 skeins (1 of each color)

Hook: 8 mm/U.S. L-11

Other: Stitch marker, yarn needle

Stitches Used

Chain stitch (ch)

Double crochet (dc)

Half double crochet (hdc)

Magic circle

Single crochet (sc)

Instructions

Make a magic circle.

Round 1: Ch 2, 10 dc in circle. Place stitch marker to indicate beg of round, and move marker up as each round is completed.

Round 2: 2 dc in each st around.

Round 3: *2 dc in next st, dc in next st; rep from * around.

Round 4: *2 dc in next st, dc in next 2 sts; rep from * around.

Round 5: *2 dc in next st, dc in next 3 sts; rep from * around.

Round 6: *2 dc in next st, dc in next 4 sts; rep from * around.

Rounds 7–9: Dc in each st around. Change color.

Round 10: Dc in each st around.

Round 11: Hdc in each st around.

Round 12: Sc in each st around. Fasten off and weave in ends.

Tip: Using a thinner yarn weight and smaller hook will create a smaller hat. You can also skip rounds 5–6 or just round 6 for a smaller hat.